Study Guide

Paul's Vision for the Deacons: Assisting the Elders with the Care of God's Church

Other books by Alexander Strauch include:

Biblical Eldership:
An Urgent Call to Restore Biblical Church Leadership

The Study Guide to Biblical Eldership:
Twelve Lessons for Mentoring Men for Eldership

Meetings That Work

The Hospitality Commands

Agape Leadership:
Lessons in Spiritual Leadership from the Life of
R. C. Chapman (Coauthored with Robert L. Peterson)

Men and Women: Equal Yet Different

A Christian Leader's Guide to Leading With Love

Love or Die:
Christ's Wake-Up Call to the Church, Revelation 2:4

If You Bite and Devour One Another:
Biblical Principles for Handling Conflict

PAUL'S VISION FOR THE
DEACONS

ASSISTING THE
ELDERS WITH
THE CARE OF
GOD'S CHURCH

ALEXANDER STRAUCH

Lewis & Roth Publishers

Paul's Vision for the Deacons: Study Guide
ISBN-10: 0936083352
ISBN-13: 9780936083353
Copyright © 2017 by Alexander Strauch. All rights reserved.

Cover design: Bryana Mansfield

Printed in the United States of America
Second Printing 2020

To receive a free catalog of books published by Lewis and Roth Publishers,
please call toll free 800-477-3239 or visit our website, *www.lewisandroth.org*.
If you are calling from outside the United States, please call 719-494-1800.

Lewis and Roth Publishers
P.O. Box 469
Littleton, Colorado 80160

CONTENTS

Chapter 1

WHAT DO DEACONS DO?

&

PAUL'S INSTRUCTIONS REGARDING DEACONS

Before completing this lesson, read the introduction, What Do Deacons Do? and Chapter 1 in *Paul's Vision for the Deacons.*

Deacons likewise must be dignified, not double-tongued, not addicted to much wine, not greedy for dishonest gain. They must hold the mystery of the faith with a clear conscience. And let them also be tested first; then let them serve as deacons if they prove themselves blameless. (1 Tim. 3:8–10)

INTRODUCTION: WHAT DO DEACONS DO?

Key Statements from "What Do Deacons Do?"

My intention in writing this book is to encourage my dear deacon friends and fellow church leaders to think more critically about what they are saying and doing in light of what Scripture actually teaches (or does not teach) about deacons. (pp. 12–13)

The Bereans . . . knew that the Scriptures were written in such a way that they must be searched and studied diligently, so they examined the Scriptures daily. (p. 14)

I am citing the attitudes and diligence of the Bereans because the nature of this biblical study of deacons requires that we do as they did. We must exert effort in order to understand and absorb the scriptural arguments presented. (p. 14)

There is another reason we need to conduct ourselves like the Bereans. It is not enough to study Scripture and discover truth. We must, by God's grace, confront our own traditions and opinions and when necessary make appropriate changes. (p. 14)

1. When you hear the word *deacons*, what comes to mind? What is your current view of the deacons' role in the church? (If you are doing this as a group study, have each person in the group share their answer.)

2. What is the stated purpose of this study?

3. List four characteristics of Berean-like Christians that you need to emulate.

4. From your list of four characteristics of Berean-like Christians, which two characteristics will be most helpful as you seek to identify the role and position of the New Testament deacon? Explain why.

5. Why do you think it is particularly important that biblical elders be Berean-like Christians? How would Berean-like elders positively affect you as deacons?

*Now these Jews were more noble
than those in Thessalonica;
They received the word with all eagerness,
examining the Scriptures daily
to see if these things were so.
Many of them therefore believed.*
Acts 17:11–12a

CHAPTER 1: PAUL'S INSTRUCTIONS REGARDING DEACONS

Key Statements from Chapter 1

Paul's gospel . . . is Christ's gospel. What Paul teaches is what Christ teaches. What Paul commands is what Christ commands. (p. 20)

One of the likely causes for the upset in Ephesus was that unqualified, unfit people had become elders and deacons during Paul's absence. (p. 22)

The overseers do not need the deacons in order to function as overseers of the local church. The *episkopoi* can stand alone, however, the deacons must stand in relationship to some person or some body of people for direction: "From the nature of the terms, *episkopoi* could operate without *diakonoi*, but *diakonoi* could not operate without some such mandating functionary as an *episkopos*."[1] (p. 25)

Paul shows as much concern for the deacons' eligibility as he does for the overseers' qualifications. (p. 26)

Unlike overseers who must be "able to teach" (1 Tim. 3:2), and "able to give instruction in sound doctrine and also to rebuke those who contradict it" (Titus 1:9), Paul does not require that deacons be "able to teach." The fact that such abilities are not required of the deacons is very important to our investigation. (p. 26)

11

We cannot account for deacon qualifications and the necessity for public examination unless deacons hold some official position of public trust or exercise some specialized ministry for which only certain people qualify. Thus there must be something very significant about the deacons' ministry that requires both specific, elder-like qualifications and verification of such qualifications by the church and its leaders. (p. 26)

One of the most critical questions in our study of deacons is: How is Paul using the Greek term *diakonos* in the two key passages? Is *diakonos* a table-servant metaphor for church officials, a commissioned messenger, or an assistant? (p. 29)

Specific Information Provided in Scripture

1. Deacons Are First Mentioned in Paul's Greeting to the Church in Philippi.
2. Deacons Are Regulated by Paul's Instructions in 1 Timothy 3:8–13.
3. Deacons Are Always Mentioned After the Overseers.
4. Deacons Are Required to Meet Specific Qualifications.
5. Deacons Are Not Required to Teach.
6. Deacons Are Required to Be Examined and Approved by the Church and Its Leaders.
7. Deacons Are Church Officeholders Like the Overseers.
8. "Deacons" Is Plural.
9. Deacons' Wives (or Women Deacons) Are Required To Meet Specific Qualifications.
10. Deacons Can Gain Much Respect in the Eyes of the Church and Have Their Faith in Christ Deepened.
11. Deacons Are Called *Diakonoi* in Greek.

NOTE: This chapter may raise many questions in your mind about deacons. You could easily get off track discussing questions that will be addressed later in the book. So do your best to confine your discussions to the questions presented here, and address other issues as they arise in the book. Don't discuss yet who deacons are according to the author, or how you will put your deacons to work.

1. Why did the author take time at this point in the book to stress that Paul is "an apostle of Christ Jesus by command of God" (1 Tim. 1:1)? List as many reasons as you can for why the author would do this.

2. Were any of the eleven points presented in Chapter 1 (see previous page) surprising or new to you? Explain your response.

3. Of the eleven points made regarding the biblical information about deacons, which three points do you find most helpful to the task of discovering what Paul teaches about the position and role of the deacons? Explain your choices.

4. How do we know that the deacons are to be subject to the overseers/elders? Why does that matter to our investigation of who deacons are and what deacons do?

5. In the opening story of this chapter, a woman asked her pastor to make her friend a deacon so that he would start attending church again. Now that you have read this chapter, how would you explain to this woman why you would not be able to fulfill her request? Do you have any Scripture to support your answer?

6. What are the three words in the *diakon-* word group? Write them out. Know their forms and practice pronouncing each of them. Say them to others in your group.

The *Diakon-* Word Group

Diakonos is pronounced dee-AH-ko-nos.

The plural form of *diakonos* is *diakonoi*, pronounced dee-AH-ko-noi.

The verb form of *diakonos* is *diakoneō*, pronounced dee-ah-ko-NEH-o.

The abstract noun form is *diakonia*, pronounced dee-ah-ko-NEE-ah.

In this study, it is important to know how to pronounce these three Greek words and to be able to distinguish the verb form, *diakoneō*, from the two noun forms, *diakonia* and *diakonos*. Greek is an inflected language that changes the form of a word depending on how it is used by an author. For simplicity and consistency, the dictionary form of each word is cited, unless otherwise noted.

---

7. What is the problem(s) we all encounter when trying to describe the role of deacons?

8. How would you answer someone who says we cannot know who the deacons are because the Bible does not provide enough information about them?

9. As a result of this biblical study of deacons, what would you personally like to see accomplished for yourself and for the church?

ADDITIONAL INFORMATION
OPTIONAL QUESTIONS AND ASSIGNMENTS

A NOTE FROM ALEXANDER STRAUCH: Throughout this guide I have included additional information, optional questions, and optional assignments. These optional exercices can be done (1) privately, (2) at the same time as the chapter questions, or (3) at your convenience after you have completed the entire book. It is your choice. A few assignments require more time and will need to be addressed after completing the study guide. My advice is, do not rush through this study guide. Take the time you need to digest thoroughly the material provided, even if that means doing two group sessions per chapter.

ASSIGNMENT

Memorize Acts 17:11.

QUESTIONS

Human Traditions Versus Direct Biblical Instructions

Be aware that many of the things that you will hear stated about deacons are merely personal opinions, preferences, assumptions, and man-made traditions. It is not uncommon to hear people make strong assertions about who deacons are without any effort whatsoever at argumentation or demonstration of biblical evidence. For instance, I presented my case for deacons being assistants to the elders to a well-known Bible teacher. I carefully presented lexical evidence from the *diakon-* word group, contextual evidence from 1 Timothy 3, and the inherent problems with the alternative views. The teacher's response was to ignore the arguments and evidence and to confidently assert that he believed that anyone serving in the church was a deacon.

Many traditional duties assigned to deacons are human traditions that are not right or wrong; they are simply traditions and ideas that have developed over time and have no scriptural basis. But they are often *treated* as scriptural principles.

We need to be aware of the difference between what Scripture actually says and what traditions people have created for deacons, e.g., deacons can only serve for three years at a time; deacons administer the Lord's Supper; deacons help with baptisms; deacons hand out the church's bulletins or usher; deacons cannot receive financial remuneration for their work. All these kinds of statements and rules (and there are many) are man-made rules and traditions that if not questioned take on the air of biblical authority.

Of course, there is nothing wrong with deacons helping with baptisms or administering the Lord's Supper (or any of these other examples). But we must be aware that these practices represent *our way* of doing things and are not necessarily deacons' responsibilities according to Scripture.

a. Why is it important to be able to distinguish man-made rules and regulations for deacons from explicit biblical instructions?

b. Why does it seem that people are more intent on holding to denominational traditions, more than to the instructions of Scripture?

> No one should become a deacon/assistant until he has been trained by the elders.

[1]John N. Collins, *Deacons and the Church* (Harrisburg, PA: Morehouse, 2002), 92.

Chapter 2

The Church Overseers, The Elders

**Before completing this lesson, read
Chapter 2 in *Paul's Vision for the Deacons*.**

This is why I left you in Crete, so that you might put what remained into order, and appoint elders in every town as I directed you—if anyone is above reproach, the husband of one wife, and his children are believers and not open to the charge of debauchery or insubordination. For an overseer, as God's steward, must be above reproach. He must not be arrogant or quick-tempered or a drunkard or violent or greedy for gain, but hospitable, a lover of good, self-controlled, upright, holy, and disciplined. He must hold firm to the trustworthy word as taught, so that he may be able to give instruction in sound doctrine and also to rebuke those who contradict it. (Titus 1:5–9)

Key Statements from Chapter 2

The Greek word for overseer is *episkopos* (pronounced, ee-PIS-ka-pos). (p. 36)

The Greek word for elder is *presbyteros* (pronounced, pres-BU-ter-os). (p. 37)

The words *overseer* and *elder* refer to the same group of officials, and the two terms are used by Paul interchangeably. Thus, any text that deals with overseers is applicable to any text that deals with elders, and vice versa. (p. 38)

Just as a household steward in Paul's day was charged with managing funds and people, God's steward must manage church resources, plan budgets, delegate tasks to others, encourage use of members' gifts, solve problems, make decisions, establish church policies, set up structures to accomplish specific work, and lead in one or more ministries of the church. Moreover, he must carefully teach the Word, judge issues and doctrines, provide counsel and education, resolve conflict among members, and care for those in the church household who cannot care for themselves. (p. 41)

The Greek word rendered "care for" (*epimeleomai*) conveys the idea of diligent, personal attention, and in this case, looking after the various needs of "God's church." As Andreas Köstenberger points out, the phrase "'*God's* church' underscores the sacredness and solemn responsibility of caring for God's people."[1] (p. 42)

Since these two preeminent New Testament apostles [Paul and Peter] charge the elders—and no other person or group—to shepherd (or in more contemporary terms, "pastor") the flock of God, we can conclude that, in biblical terms, the elders are responsible for the pastoral oversight of the local church. (p. 44)

An elder must have the ability to teach and defend sound doctrine, which is not required of the deacon. (p. 44)

A biblical eldership is not a passive, ineffective, uninvolved committee, but a Spirit-appointed body of qualified, functioning shepherds who jointly pastor God's flock. In biblical terms, the elders are the overseers, shepherds, stewards, teachers, and leaders of the local church. They are men who desire to care for God's church and who are above reproach in character, knowledgeable in Scripture, sound in doctrine, able to teach the Word and to protect the church from false teachers. (p. 47)

---

1. Why do the deacons need to know the biblical roles and identity of the New Testament overseers? Why is this important to know, as you go forward in this study?

2. What ideas are conveyed by the title *episkopos*?

21

3. Can you give any biblical proof that overseers are the same group of officials called elders? Why is this important?

4. Why does Paul refer to "overseers" in the plural in Acts 20:28 and Philippians 1:1, and to "the overseer" in the singular in 1 Timothy 3:2 and Titus 1:7? (See endnote 3 on page 49 in the text.) Why is it important to be able to answer this question correctly?

5. What are the different nuances of the terms "overseer" and "elder" when used of the same group of officials?

6. What does the phrase "God's steward" (Titus 1:7) tell you about the biblical concept of the position and work of the overseers (= elders)?

7. What does the phrase "care for God's church" tell you about the work of the overseers/elders (1 Tim. 3:5)? To help you answer this question, see Luke 10:34 where the same Greek word for "care" (*epimeleomai*) is used.

8. One of the most beautiful and significant images in the Bible is the image of the sheep and the shepherd. The Lord is our Shepherd (Ps. 23:1). Jesus is the Good Shepherd and we are his purchased sheep (John 10:11). The Spirit of God charges the elders "to shepherd the church of God" (Acts 20:28). What does Acts 20:28 tell you about the position, authority, and work of the overseers/elders in the church?

9. List all that Christian elders are expected to do according to Acts 20:26–31. Why is it essential to the deacons' work to understand the full shepherding task God has given to the church elders?

10. In what ways do Peter and Paul agree about the identity and work of the elders (Acts 20:28–31; 1 Peter 5:1–2)? What new truths about shepherd elders does Peter add to Paul's teachings?

11. What vitally important instruction does 1 Timothy 5:17–18 give to the local church and its elders? Be sure you understand this significant passage of Scripture.

> Let the elders who rule well be considered worthy of double honor, especially those who labor in preaching and teaching. For the Scripture says, "You shall not muzzle an ox when it treads out the grain," and, "The laborer deserves his wages." (1 Tim. 5:17–18)

12. What does it mean that the elders "must help the weak"? Why would this injunction be important to elders and deacons?

> In all things I have shown you that by working hard in this way we must help the weak and remember the words of the Lord Jesus, how he himself said, "It is more blessed to give than to receive." (Acts 20:35)

13. In what ways has your understanding of the biblical term elders changed as a result of reading Chapter 2?

ADDITIONAL INFORMATION
OPTIONAL QUESTIONS AND ASSIGNMENTS

ASSIGNMENT

Memorize Acts 20:28.

QUESTIONS

The Terminology Battle
A deeply rooted problem we all must encounter is the definition of the term *elder*. Although the term *elder* is the predominant New Testament term used to describe local church leaders . . . Most people think of church elders as lay, church-board members who are separate and distinct from the professional,

ordained pastor (or clergyman). I refer to these elders as "board elders;" they are not true biblical elders. They are advisers, committee men, executives, and directors. Their term in office is of a limited duration.

A true biblical eldership is not a businesslike committee. It's a biblically qualified council of men that jointly pastors the local church. So to communicate the New Testament idea of eldership, we need to reeducate ourselves as to the New Testament usage of the term *elder*, and in some cases choose a different term.

If we choose to use the term *elder*, which many Protestant churches do because it is a key biblical term for church leaders, it is necessary to explain that the term *elders* means "pastor elders," "shepherd elders," or "pastors." . . . I use these descriptions in order to distinguish between "board elders," which is a misleading concept, and "shepherd elders," which is the biblical concept. In some churches the term *elder* is used in its full New Testament sense, thus the need to search for another term doesn't exist. The people in these churches know that the elders are their spiritual leaders, but this is true of very few churches.

I know some churches that sought to implement a biblical eldership but weren't able to make it work effectively until they dropped the term *elder* and called their elders "pastors." In these churches the term *elder* was so deeply entangled with temporary, committee-board connotations that the term was a hindrance to the practice of biblical eldership. Even the elders were helped by the language change. They started thinking of themselves as pastors who were responsible for the spiritual care of the flock and began to function as pastors. Despite the clerical and professional connotations of the term *pastor*, it best communicated what the church wanted to say about their elders' function and position.

Many times I use the word *shepherd* because it does not carry all the unbiblical connotations that people usually associate with the terms *pastor* or *elder*. However, even the term *shepherd*, like all the

*Whoever closes his ear to the cry
of the poor will himself call out
and not be answered.*

Proverbs 21:13

other terms, has its own problems: It is a word devoid of religious meaning for most people outside the church, and some inside as well. Some people might think you are referring to a literal shepherd and may want to know where your farm is located!

Whatever terminology you choose to describe local church leaders will have advantages and disadvantages. In the end, every local church is responsible to teach its people the meaning of the terms it uses to describe its spiritual leaders, whether it be elders, overseers, ministers, preachers, or pastors. Biblically sensitive church leaders will insist that the terminology they use represents, as accurately as possible, the original biblical terms and concepts of a New Testament eldership (Adapted from *Biblical Eldership: An Urgent Call to Restore Biblical Church Leadership*).

Most churches refer to *the* pastor and the elders separately. But this is not a biblical distinction; the false pastor-elders distinction demeans the concept of biblical eldership and causes more eldership confusion.

a. Why does the terminology you use for your church's leaders matter to your church and its leaders?

b. Why is it important that you distinguish between "board elders" and "shepherd elders"?

c. What do you think the term *elders* convey to the people of your church?

d. What changes do you think need to be made to improve your church's leadership terminology?

Suggested Reading

If you would like more information about New Testament, Christian elders you can read my explanation in *Biblical Eldership: An Urgent Call to Restore Biblical Church Leadership* (Littleton, CO: Lewis and Roth, 1995) or *Biblical Eldership: Restoring the Eldership to its Rightful Place in the Church* (this is a 47-page pamphlet summarizing the full book *Biblical Eldership*).

Also, I highly recommend Biblical Eldership Resources (www.biblicaleldership.com) for additional materials on biblical eldership. This website is designed for training future pastor elders and for helping present elders be more effective in their pastoral ministry. In addition, the website guides churches that want to develop a biblical eldership model of leadership and governance. For a specific explanation of the concept of biblical eldership, go to http://biblicaleldership.com/what-biblical-eldership-0/restoring-biblical-eldership.

If you are a student of Scripture and enjoy reading, I highly recommend Dr. Joseph Hellerman's book, *Embracing Shared Ministry: Power and Status in the Early Church and Why It Matters Today* (Kregel, 2013).

To help you understand the biblical image of a shepherd and his work with sheep, I highly recommend reading:

W. Phillip Keller, *A Shepherd Looks at Psalm 23* (Zondervan, 2007)

W. Phillip Keller, *The Shepherd Trilogy* (Zondervan, 1996) (This volume includes the first book mentioned, as well as two others.)

Biblical References to Elders

And [the Christians in Antioch] did so, sending [their charitable offering] to the elders by the hand of Barnabas and Saul. (Acts 11:30)

And when they [Paul and Barnabas] had appointed elders for them in every church, with prayer and fasting they committed them to the Lord in whom they had believed. (Acts 14:23)

And after Paul and Barnabas had no small dissension and debate with them, Paul and Barnabas and some of the others were appointed to go up to Jerusalem to the apostles and the elders about this question...When they came to Jerusalem, they were welcomed by the church and the apostles and the elders, and they declared all that God had done with them . . . The apostles and the elders were gathered together to consider this matter. (Acts 15:2, 4, 6)

Then it seemed good to the apostles and the elders, with the whole church, to choose men from among them and send them to Antioch with Paul and Barnabas. They sent Judas called Barsabbas, and Silas, leading men among the brothers, with the following letter: "The brothers, both the apostles and the elders, to the brothers who are of the Gentiles in Antioch and Syria and Cilicia, greetings." (Acts 15:22–23)

As they went on their way through the cities, they delivered to them for observance the decisions that had been reached by the apostles and elders who were in Jerusalem. (Acts 16:4)

Now from Miletus he sent to Ephesus and called the elders of the church to come to him . . . "[You elders] pay careful attention to yourselves and to all the flock, in which the Holy Spirit has made you overseers, to care for the church of God, which he obtained with his own blood. I know that after my departure fierce wolves will come in among you, not sparing the flock; and from among your own selves will arise men speaking twisted things, to draw away the disciples after them. Therefore be alert, remembering that for three years I did not cease night or day to admonish every one with tears. And now I commend you to God and to the word of his grace, which is able to build you up and to give you the inheritance among all those who are sanctified. I coveted no one's silver or gold or apparel. You yourselves know that these hands ministered to my necessities and to those who were with me. In all things I have shown you that by working hard in this way we must help the weak and remember the words of the Lord Jesus, how he himself said, 'It is more blessed to give than to receive.'" (Acts 20:17, 28–35)

Paul and Timothy, servants of Christ Jesus, to all the saints in Christ Jesus who are at Philippi, with the overseers and deacons. (Phil. 1:1)

The saying is trustworthy: If anyone aspires to the office of overseer, he desires a noble task. Therefore an overseer must be above reproach, the husband of one wife, sober-minded, self-controlled, respectable, hospitable, able to teach, not a drunkard, not violent but gentle, not quarrelsome, not a lover of money. He must manage his own household well, with all dignity keeping his children submissive, for if someone does not know how to manage his own household, how will he care for God's church? He must not be a recent convert, or he may become puffed up with conceit and fall into the condemnation of the devil. Moreover, he must be well thought of by outsiders, so that he may not fall into disgrace, into a snare of the devil. (1 Tim. 3:1–7)

Do not neglect the gift you have, which was given you by prophecy when the council of elders laid their hands on you. (1 Tim. 4:14)

Let the elders who rule well be considered worthy of double honor, especially those who labor in preaching and teaching. For the Scripture says, "You shall not muzzle an ox when it treads out the grain," and, "The laborer deserves his wages." Do not admit a charge against an elder except on the evidence of two or three witnesses. As for those who persist in sin, rebuke them in the presence of all, so that the rest may stand in fear. In the presence of God and of Christ Jesus and of the elect angels I charge you to keep these rules without prejudging, doing nothing from partiality. Do not be hasty in the laying on of hands, nor take part in the sins of others; keep yourself pure. (No longer drink only water, but use a little wine for the sake of your stomach and your frequent ailments.) The sins of some people are conspicuous, going before them to judgment, but the sins of others appear later. So also good works are conspicuous, and even those that are not cannot remain hidden. (1 Tim. 5:17–25)

This is why I left you in Crete, so that you might put what remained into order, and appoint elders in every town as I directed you— if anyone is above reproach, the husband of one wife, and his children are believers and not open to the charge of debauchery or insubordination. For an overseer, as God's steward, must be above reproach. He must not be arrogant or quick-tempered or a drunkard or violent or greedy for gain, but hospitable, a lover of good, self-controlled, upright, holy, and disciplined. He must hold firm to the trustworthy word as taught, so that he may be able to give instruction in sound doctrine and also to rebuke those who contradict it. (Titus 1:5–9)

Is anyone among you sick? Let him call for the elders of the church, and let them pray over him, anointing him with oil in the name of the Lord. And the prayer of faith will save the one who is sick, and the Lord will raise him up. And if he has committed sins, he will be forgiven. (James 5:14–15)

So I exhort the elders among you, as a fellow elder and a witness of the sufferings of Christ, as well as a partaker in the glory that is going to be revealed: shepherd the flock of God that is among you, exercising oversight, not under compulsion, but willingly, as God would have you; not for shameful gain, but eagerly; not domineering over those in your charge, but being examples to the flock. And when the chief Shepherd appears, you will receive the unfading crown of glory. Likewise, you who are younger, be subject to the elders. Clothe yourselves, all of you, with humility toward one another, for "God opposes the proud but gives grace to the humble." (1 Peter 5:1–5)

> **For full expositions of Acts 20 and 1 Peter 5,**
> **visit www.biblicaleldership.com.**

---

[1] *Biblical Theology for Christian Proclamation: Commentary on 1–2 Timothy & Titus* (Nashville, TN: B&H, 2017), 130.

Chapter 3

Deacons, Assistants to the Elders

> **Before completing this lesson, read
> Chapter 3 in *Paul's Vision for the Deacons*.**

Paul and Timothy, servants of Christ Jesus,
To all the saints in Christ Jesus who are at Philippi, with the overseers and deacons. (Phil. 1:1)

Key Statements from Chapter 3

Of the twenty-one occurrences of *diakonos* in Paul's letters, the *English Standard Version* transliterates only three of them as "deacons" (Phil. 1:1; 1 Tim. 3:8, 12). (p. 51)

As a result of his research, [Dr. Clarence D. Agan III] proposes four uses of the *diakon-* word group: Table attendance, domestic attendance, communication or delivery, agency or instrumentality. (pp. 53–54)

Paul is not using the term *diakonos* to mean a servant in a general, undefined sense that could apply to any Christian. (p. 55)

The key to understanding the deacons of 1 Timothy 3:8–13 is to accurately understand the officials with whom they are associated: that is, the overseer, superintendent, supervisor, or guardian. (p. 56)

The deacons are not a separate, autonomous body of officials disconnected from the body of overseers. As the context and the terms themselves indicate, the *diakonoi* operate under the leadership of the *episkopoi*. (p. 57)

The title "assistants" describes instantly who the deacons are and what they do without elaborate explanation or assumptions that are not biblically provable, e.g., "exemplary servants," "leading servants," or "table servants." (pp. 58–59)

The critical qualification that an overseer/elder "be able to give instruction in sound doctrine and also to rebuke those who contradict it" (Titus 1:9) is *not* required of deacons. This is not an accidental omission on Paul's part. (p. 62)

NOTE: In this chapter, and in several others, I refer you to my website (www.deaconbook.com) for additional material. I did this in order to keep this book from becoming too large and overloaded with weighty, technical details. This book could easily have become three hundred plus pages, and few people would have read it. I hope, however, that in the future you will read the extra material at your leisure.

1. On a scale of 1 to 5 (1 being easy and 5 being very difficult), how difficult was Chapter 3 for you to understand? Discuss your answer with the group.

Easy 1 ———— 2———— 3———— 4————5 Very Difficult

2. What point(s) presented in Chapter 3 was most difficult for you to understand? Discuss this matter with your group or mentor. What needs to occur for you to be sure you grasp the arguments of this chapter?

3. The critical issue in identifying the New Testament deacon is this: How is Paul using the Greek word *diakonos* in 1 Timothy 3:8-13 and Philippians 1:1? Clarence Agan identifies four uses of the *diakon-* word group (see pages 53–54 in the text). Using the verses below, identify which one of the four usages of the *diakon-* word group matches the verses.

a. Romans 13:4

b. 2 Corinthians 3:3

c. Luke 17:7–8

d. Matthew 25:44

e. Ephesians 3:7–9

f. Acts 19:22

g. John 2:9

4. There are five points under the heading, Evidence for Deacons as Assistants (see pages 52–61 in the text). Which two points do you think present the strongest evidence that deacons are assistants to the elders? Explain your answers.

5. Explain the point of the second argument, Eliminating Alternative Usages of *Diakonos*, for supporting the view that deacons are assistants to the elders (see pages 54–56 in the text).

6. What does the author mean when he says, "Not every use of *diakonos* means simply 'servant' or carries menial, servile connotations"? Why is this an important point to grasp?

7. List the facts that demonstrate that the overseers are the supervisors of the deacons.

8. Why is the simplicity of the interpretation of *diakonos* as "assistant" a very strong argument in its favor?

9. Why would Paul want the elders to have officially recognized assistants? List as many reasons as you can.

10. List potential problems associated with the assistants-to-the-elders view.

We began the book with the Berean Challenge. "They [the Bereans] received the word with all eagerness, examining the Scriptures daily to see if these things we so. Many of them therefore believed" (Acts 17:11–12a).

Chapter 3 will require Berean-like motivation and determination to understand the arguments presented. It is possible that the Bereans examined the Scriptures together to see if Paul's claims about Jesus the Messiah were true. It might help if you examine the arguments of this chapter together with other Bereans.

11. How would you describe the biblical relationship between the deacons and the church elders?

12. In what specific ways can an elder abuse the policy of deacons acting as assistants to the elders?

13. I have talked to many deacons who are uncertain about their position in the church and what they are to do. Why is it important for the deacons to be perfectly clear about their position in the church and what they are to do?

Additional Information
Optional Questions and Assignments

Assignment

Memorize Philippians 1:1.

Questions

Is Bob a Deacon or a Servant?
Bob is retired from work for medical reasons. He uses most of his time to serve his local church. Before each church meeting,

seven days a week, Bob arrives early to set up chairs and tables, adjust the thermostat, and prepare snacks and drinks. Afterward, Bob puts away the tables and chairs, vacuums, removes trash, and locks up the building. At times, other church members help Bob set up and clean up, but on many occasions he does his tasks alone without complaint. He works cheerfully throughout the week without expecting financial compensation.

Bob is a faithful servant of the church. But is Bob a deacon?

The people in Bob's church say, "Of course Bob is a deacon!" They say this because they believe that the Greek word for deacon (*diakonos*) simply means "servant" and nothing more.[1] Thus anyone regularly serving others is a servant (*diakonos*), and consequently, considered a deacon.

However, based on the New Testament criteria, Bob is not a deacon. Setting up tables, cleaning up after meetings, and making coffee is not necessarily the work of deacons. But there is another matter to consider: Bob does not meet the biblical qualifications to be a deacon. Bob does not manage his own household well and there are other problems in his life that disqualify him from being a deacon.

Yet, Bob's name is listed in the church bulletin as a deacon. Many in Bob's church insist that Bob is a deacon. They do not take seriously the biblical qualifications for deacons. They may say they do, but in practice they do not. They consider Bob to be a deacon because of all the work that he does in the church.

To be clear, Bob is a servant in the functional, gifted sense, but not a servant in the formal officeholder sense of the word as used by Paul. I do not want to diminish Bob's exemplary service to the body of Christ. He is engaged in doing the "good works" which God has prepared for him (Eph. 2:10). But he is not a biblical deacon.

a. What does this story tell you about what many people think about deacons?

b. If Bob is not a deacon, what is his role in the local church? How would you describe him and his ministry?

c. How does Ephesians 4:11–12 (and Eph. 2:10) help us to understand the above account about Bob?

Christ's Teachings on Humble Servant Leadership
To serve as an assistant to the elders as God would have you, you must know and practice our Lord's unique teaching on humble servant leadership. Read and internalize the following passages of Scripture:

Matt. 11:29: Gentle and Humble
Take my yoke upon you, and learn from me, for I am gentle and lowly in heart, and you will find rest for your souls.

a. In your own words, explain Jesus' description of himself. In what ways would Jesus' own self-description affect your attitude and work as a deacon?

Matt. 23:1–12: The Humble Shall Be Exalted

Then Jesus said to the crowds and to his disciples, "The scribes and the Pharisees sit on Moses' seat, so do and observe whatever they tell you, but not the works they do. For they preach, but do not practice. They tie up heavy burdens, hard to bear, and lay them on people's shoulders, but they themselves are not willing to move them with their finger. They do all their deeds to be seen by others. For they make their phylacteries broad and their fringes long, and they love the place of honor at feasts and the best seats in the synagogues and greetings in the marketplaces and being called rabbi by others. But you are not to be called rabbi, for you have one teacher, and you are all brothers. And call no man your father on earth, for you have one Father, who is in heaven. Neither be called instructors, for you have one instructor, the Christ. The greatest among you shall be your servant. Whoever exalts himself will be humbled, and whoever humbles himself will be exalted."

b. The above passage is a very important passage. It contrasts the common religious mindset of pride and selfishness with the new mindset of Jesus (Phil. 2:5) and his followers. How would you describe this new mindset (attitude, disposition) which should characterize all deacons and elders?

Mark 9:33–35: Humble Servants of All

And they came to Capernaum. And when he was in the house he asked them, "What were you discussing on the way?" But they kept silent, for on the way they had argued with one another about who was the greatest. And he sat down and called the twelve. And he said to them, "If anyone would be first, he must be last of all and servant of all."

c. In this passage, Jesus makes a paradoxical statement regarding those who lead in his kingdom. Jesus' teaching regarding leadership and the use of authority has a completely different orientation than the world's model of leadership. What does Jesus mean by the term "first"? What does he mean by the phrases "last of all" and "servant of all"? How do you explain this paradoxical statement?

Mark 10:35–45: Sacrifice, Service, and Suffering

And James and John, the sons of Zebedee, came up to him and said to him, "Teacher, we want you to do for us whatever we ask of you." And he said to them, "What do you want me to do for you?" And they said to him, "Grant us to sit, one at your right hand and one at your left, in your glory." Jesus said to them, "You do not know what you are asking. Are you able to drink the cup that I drink, or to be baptized with the baptism with which I am baptized?" And they said to him, "We are able." And Jesus said to them, "The cup that I drink you will drink, and with the baptism with which I am baptized, you will be baptized, but to sit at my right hand or at my left is not mine to grant, but it is for those for whom it has been prepared." And when the ten heard it, they began to be indignant at James and John. And Jesus called them to him and said to them, "You know that those who are considered rulers of the Gentiles lord it over them, and their great ones exercise authority over them. But it shall not be so among you. But whoever would be great among you must be your servant, and whoever would be first among you must be slave of all. For even the Son of Man came not to be served but to serve, and to give his life as a ransom for many."

d. List a few key differences between the world's style of leadership and use of leadership authority, and Jesus' new style of leadership and the exercise of leadership authority in Jesus' kingdom.

Luke 22:24–27: One Who Serves

A dispute also arose among them, as to which of them was to be regarded as the greatest. And he said to them, "The kings of the Gentiles exercise lordship over them, and those in authority over them are called benefactors. But not so with you. Rather, let the greatest among you become as the youngest, and the leader as one who serves. For who is the greater, one who reclines at table or one who serves? Is it not the one who reclines at table? But I am among you as the one who serves."

e. How would this passage affect your thinking about yourself as a deacon? How would it affect your relationship with the elders?

John 13:3–17: Washing One Another's Feet

Jesus, knowing that the Father had given all things into his hands, and that he had come from God and was going back to God, rose from supper. He laid aside his outer garments, and taking a towel, tied it around his waist. Then he poured water into a basin and began to wash the disciples' feet and to wipe them with the towel that was wrapped around him. He came to Simon Peter, who said to him, "Lord, do you wash my feet?" Jesus answered him, "What I am doing you do not understand now, but afterward you will understand." Peter said to him, "You shall never wash my feet." Jesus answered him, "If I do not wash you, you have no share with me." Simon Peter said to him, "Lord, not my feet only but also my hands and my head!" Jesus said to him, "The one who has bathed does not need to wash, except for his feet, but is completely clean. And you are clean, but not every one of you." For he knew who was to betray him; that was why he said, "Not all of you are clean."

When he had washed their feet and put on his outer garments and resumed his place, he said to them, "Do you understand what I have done to you? You call me Teacher and Lord, and you are right, for so I am. If I then, your Lord and Teacher, have washed your feet, you also ought to wash one another's feet. For I have given you an example, that you also should do just as I have done to you. Truly, truly, I say to you, a servant is not greater than his master, nor is a messenger greater than the one who sent him. If you know these things, blessed are you if you do them."

f. Give a few examples of how we would wash one another's feet today. Be specific. What would this look like in practice?

John 13:34–35: Love

"A new commandment I give to you, that you love one another: just as I have loved you, you also are to love one another. By this all people will know that you are my disciples, if you have love for one another."

g. What is the difference between the new commandment and the Old Testament commandment to "love your neighbor as yourself" (Lev. 19:18)?

---

[1]Joe McKeever, "12 Things I Tell the Deacons," http://joemckeever.com/wp/12-deacons/.

Chapter 4

Assisting the Elders with the Care of God's Church

Before completing this lesson, read Chapter 4 in *Paul's Vision for the Deacons*.

The twelve summoned the full number of the disciples and said, "It is not right that we should give up preaching the word of God to serve tables . . . we will devote ourselves to prayer and to the ministry of the word." (Acts 6:2, 4)

Key Statements from Chapter 4

> From the post-apostolic literature of the next three centuries [after the Acts 6 account], we see that the deacons became closely associated with the church's charitable relief work. They were regularly (but not exclusively) associated with the care of the poor and the sick and the distribution of charitable gifts. (p. 73)

> Unlike the table-serving officials of Acts 6, Paul's *diakonoi* are not limited to charitable ministries, even if care for the poor and the sick became a major part of their responsibilities, as is likely. (p. 74)

> The specific tasks of the deacons are to be determined by the elders in accordance with the church's particular needs, size, and giftedness of its members. (p. 74)

> Deacons work directly at helping the elders . . . They are, as their title states, *assistants*. (p. 76)

> Not everyone who leads a church ministry is an assistant of the elders. Nor should the whole church body be construed to be elders' assistants. (p. 76)

---

1. Acts 6:1–7 is full of invaluable biblical principles (truths, lessons) for guiding the priorities of a local church, including its elders and deacons. From the text below, list as many of these key principles as you can. You can divide your answers into groups: principles for elders and deacons, and principles for the church as a whole. (For a detailed exposition of Acts 6:1–7, go to www.deaconbook.com.)

Now in these days when the disciples were increasing in number, a complaint by the Hellenists arose against the Hebrews because their widows were being neglected in the daily distribution. And the twelve summoned the full number of the disciples and said, "It is not right that we should give up preaching the word of God to serve tables. Therefore, brothers, pick out from among you seven men of good repute, full of the Spirit and of wisdom, whom we will appoint to this duty. But we will devote ourselves to prayer and to the ministry of the word." And what they said pleased the whole gathering, and they chose Stephen, a man full of faith and of the Holy Spirit, and Philip, and Prochorus, and Nicanor, and Timon, and Parmenas, and Nicolaus, a proselyte of Antioch. These they set before the apostles, and they prayed and laid their hands on them. And the word of God continued to increase, and the number of the disciples multiplied greatly in Jerusalem, and a great many of the priests became obedient to the faith. (Acts 6:1–7)

2. If you are a pastor elder in a church, what would be the one indispensable principle you should learn from Acts 6 and never forget? Deacons should answer this question also.

3. Although Acts 6 is most likely not an account of appointment of the first deacons, what major lesson should deacons take from this account and apply to themselves as aides to the elders?

4. Why would the care of widows and the poor be a natural fit for the role of the deacons/assistants?

5. List some of the official tasks that the deacons can carry out on behalf of the elders. Specifically, what kinds of tasks would elders need special assistance with, in order to free them to focus more effectively on leading and teaching? List as many as you can.

The Necessity of Good Management in God's Household

Good management of funds and resources is essential if any organization is to maintain integrity, effectiveness, and growth. Disorganization or mismanagement always significantly multiplies problems and frustrates people. It ruins families, businesses, governments, and churches. It is the product of the polluted soil of laziness, thoughtlessness, procrastination, and selfishness. It is not from God.

Therefore, the local church should not be mismanaged by its leaders. God should receive our best effort, energy, and skill (2 Cor. 8:20–21). The entire account of Acts 6 is an example of good church leadership, organization, delegation, and loving care for the people of God. A successful deacons' ministry is based on good organization, effective communication, and clear delegation on the part of the elders.

6. As stated on the next page, "A successful deacons' ministry is dependent largely on effective supervision by the elders." If you are the elders of the church, in what specific ways can you organize and regularly guide the deacons in their service?

7. Why do you think deacons are not mentioned in Titus 1:5–10?

8. Explain the doctrine of every-member ministry in the body of Christ. What biblical texts teach this amazing Christian doctrine? When defining the role of the deacons, why must the doctrine of every-member ministry be kept in mind at all times? For further information on the biblical doctrine of every-member ministry in the body of Christ, go to www.deaconbook.com.

9. Why would deacons need to meet together as a deliberative body? List as many reasons as you can. Why would deacons not need to meet together as a deliberative body?

> Deacons work directly at helping the elders, relieving them of certain administrative and pastoral tasks. They are, as their title states, *assistants*.

A successful deacons' ministry is dependent largely on effective supervision by the elders. As many questions about deacons are not answered in Scripture, the elders have a great deal of flexibility in how to direct and utilize them. The elders need to use their God-given creative thinking powers and organizational skills to effectively utilize the ministry of deacons. If not, the deacons will flounder and become frustrated with the elders.

Paul's Vision for the Deacons, page 76

10. How do the following Scripture passages guide the deacons in their relationships with the elders and the congregation?

a. Galatians 5:19–23

b. 1 Peter 5:5

c. Philippians 2:3–8

d. Hebrews 13:17

e. 1 Thessalonians 5:12–13

f. 1 Corinthians 12:31–13:3

g. 1 Corinthians 16:14

11. What do you think will happen if the deacons are not diligent in their work, or do not take initiative, or do not follow through with their responsibilities? List three adverse consequences.

When accountability lessens, responsibility lessens.

ADDITIONAL INFORMATION
OPTIONAL QUESTIONS AND ASSIGNMENTS

ASSIGNMENTS

Memorize Acts 6:4.

Design a Job Description

Consider having a written job description for each deacon. It will be especially helpful if the job description includes not only deacon-related responsibilities, but also other non-deacon ministries and responsibilities. This would clarify for the other deacons and the elders the extent of the deacon's involvement within the church. Having a deacon's responsibilities and obligations clearly outlined could also save him from over-extending himself in ministry. This job description should be reviewed each year by the elders and deacons.

Some Basic Principles of Effective Communication

Bruce Stabbert writes, "One of the most essential ingredients of any kind of teamwork is good communications."[3] Yet in many cases, poor communication exists among members of the eldership council, between the elders and the congregation, and between the elders and deacons. Faulty communication has many detrimental effects:

- Vague delegation of responsibilities, resulting in duplication and overlap
- Failure to respond to people's requests and questions
- Lack of follow-through on group tasks
- Misunderstanding, suspicion, and isolation among various team members
- Hesitancy to direct or correct one another
- Failure to instruct or support people in fulfilling their responsibilities
- Poor morale among team members
- People routinely being hurt

As a leader of people, be concerned about improving your ability to communicate. God is verbal and created us to be verbal creatures. We were made to communicate with God and people, but the Fall impaired this wondrous gift. Sin distorts our ability to communicate, creating many interpersonal problems. Poor communication causes unnecessary frustrations in a congregation. Here are some basic principles for improving your communication.

- Be aware that skillful communication is hard work.
- Be aware of the ways you block good communication.
- Make a conscious effort to be a patient listener.
- Learn to speak gently, calmly, graciously, and tactfully.
- Be sure to clarify responsibilities and work assignments.
- Provide adequate instruction when you give a person a job.
- Don't spring important decisions on people.
- Speak words of encouragement more than words of correction.

(For more information on each of these principles, see Alexander Strauch, *Meetings That Work: A Guide to Effective Elders' Meetings* [Littleton, CO: Lewis and Roth, 2001], 33–40.)

a. An effective elder-deacon working relationship is based on frequent, open communication. If you are the elders of the church, how can you continue to improve your communication with the deacons?

b. If you are the deacons, how can you continue to improve your communication with the elders?

Suggested Reading

On the issue of handling conflict, an important book for all elders and deacons is *If You Bite and Devour One Another: Biblical Principles for Handling Conflict*, by Alexander Strauch. It is an essential book for every member of your church.

The question arises: Should deacons attend the elders' meetings regularly, occasionally, or not at all? This is a matter that should be decided by the elders. The deacons do need to know and understand the thinking of the elders on some of the issues they (the deacons) are dealing with. This will allow the deacons to assist the elders more effectively. The issue is, there needs to be <u>good communication</u> between elders and deacons so the deacons can do their work effectively.

That's Not My Job

This is a story about four people name Everybody, Somebody, Anybody, and Nobody.
There was an important job to be done and Everybody was sure that Somebody would do it.
Anybody could have done it, but Nobody did it.
Somebody got angry about that, because it was Everybody's job.
Everybody thought Anybody could do it, but Nobody realized that Everybody wouldn't do it.
It end up that Everybody blamed Somebody when Nobody did what Anybody could have done.

---

[1]John Stott, *The Living Church: Convictions of a Lifelong Pastor* (Downers Grove, IL: IVP Books, 2007), 76.
[2]Andrew D. Clarke, *A Pauline Theology of Church Leadership* (New York: Bloomsbury, 2008), 136.
[3]Bruce Stabbert, *The Team Concept: Paul's Church Leadership Pattern or Ours?* (Tacoma, WA: Hegg, 1982), 177.

Chapter 5

The Deacons' Qualifications

1 Timothy 3:8–9

> Before completing this lesson, read
> Chapter 5 in *Paul's Vision for the Deacons.*

Deacons likewise must be dignified, not double-tongued, not addicted to much wine, not greedy for dishonest gain. They must hold the mystery of the faith with a clear conscience. (1 Tim. 3:8–9)

Key Statements from Chapter 5

Scripture makes the uncontested point that God's paramount concern is not with buildings or programs but with the moral and spiritual character of those who lead his people. (p. 87)

[Paul] knew that the devil would use any failing on the part of the church's leaders to shame the church's public image. So, to protect the credibility of the gospel and the reputation of the local church from public ridicule, Paul insisted that the church's elders and deacons "be above reproach," morally and spiritually. (pp. 88–89)

In the Lord's work, a leader's moral character and public reputation are essential to the task of leading God's people. (p. 89)

[The term "dignified"] describes a person whose attitudes and conduct win the admiration of others. It refers to a respectable, well-thought-of person. (pp. 89–90)

The word "double-tongued" or "double-worded" (*dilogos*) expresses the idea of saying one thing to one person and saying something different to another. So this qualification emphasizes integrity of speech and specifically prohibits any kind of "insincere"[1] or duplicitous speech. (p. 91)

We cannot be naïve about the temptations church leaders face. Stealing church donations or misappropriating church funds is a widespread problem. Even among the twelve disciples there was a thief. (p. 97)

The New Testament does not allow believers to separate life and doctrine. It requires consistency between belief and practice. However, some professing Christians claim to hold to orthodox doctrine but *exhibit* unorthodox thinking and behavior. (p. 100)

---

1. After reading the quotation by Jerome (see page 87 in the text), do you see his complaint as having any relevance for today's churches? If so, explain or give an example.

2. What specific concern did Paul have in mind that compelled him to establish the moral and spiritual qualifications for both elders and deacons (1 Tim. 3:1–13)?

3. The first qualification for a deacon is "dignified" (1 Tim. 3:8). In your own words, explain what the term *dignified* requires of a deacon candidate. Why do you think this qualification begins the list of deacon qualifications?

A good name is to be chosen rather than great riches, and favor is better than silver or gold. (Prov. 22:1)

A good name is better than precious ointment. (Ecc. 1:1)

4. Why is integrity of speech an essential biblical requirement for a deacon? List as many reasons as you can.

What the Bible says about integrity of speech and lying:

Lev. 19:11; Num. 23:19; Deut. 5:20; Ps. 5:6; 10:7; 34:13; 50:19–20; 52:1–4; 64; 120; Prov. 6:12–19; 12:17–22; 15:1–7; 20:25; 21:23; 24:28; Jer. 9:3–9; Zec. 8:16–17; Matt. 5:37; John 8:42–46; Eph. 4:15, 25; Col. 3:9–10; James 3:1–12; 5:12; 1 Peter 3:10; Rev. 21:8; 22:15.

Righteous lips are the delight of a king, and he loves him who speaks what is right. (Prov. 16:13)

5. What does Ecclesiastes 10:1 mean and how would you apply it to the prohibition of "not double-tongued"?

Dead flies make the perfumer's ointment give off a stench; so a little folly outweighs wisdom and honor. (Eccl. 10:1)

6. How would you be able to identify a person who is a "closet alcoholic" or a "high-functioning alcoholic"? How would you "care-front" such a person?

7. In what subtle ways can church leaders misappropriate money for one's own profit?

Addictions Among Church Leaders

Alcohol abuse among Christians is a problem. In a survey done by Pepperdine University and the Barna Group, a well-known church research organization, it is estimated that some 17 percent of pastors struggle with addiction to alcohol or prescription drugs (*Christianity Today*, September 2016, 18). Such addictions may be a bigger problem among church leaders than we realize.

Biblical warning about the abuse of wine and strong drink:

Gen. 9:20–27; 19:30–34; Prov. 20:1; 23:20–21, 30–35; 26:9–10; 31:4–5; Eccl. 10:17; Isa. 5:11, 22–23; 28:7–8; Hos. 4:11; Rom. 13:13; 1 Cor. 5:11; 6:9–10; Gal. 5:19–21; Eph. 5:18; 1 Thess. 5:7–8; Titus 1:7; 1 Peter 4:3.

[Writing to the Corinthians about delivering the Gentile offering for the poor Christians in Jerusalem, Paul says]

"We take this course so that
no one should blame us
about this generous gift
that is being administered by us,
for we aim at what is honorable
not only in the Lord's sight
but also in the sight of man."

2 Corinthians 8:20–21

Biblical warning about stealing and greed:

Ex. 20:15, 17; Lev. 19:11; Num. 22–24; 1 Sam. 2:13–17; 8:3; 2 Kings 5:20–27; Neh. 6:10–14; Prov. 21:17; Eccl. 5:10; Isa. 22:15–25; 56:9–11; Ezek. 22:25, 27; Mic. 2:2; 3:11; Matt. 6:24; 21:13; 23:25; Luke 11:39; 16:13; John 2:13–17; Acts 8:9–24; 1 Cor. 6:10; Eph. 4:28; 1 Tim. 3:3; 6:10; Heb. 13:5; James 4:2; 5:1–6; 1 Peter 4:15; 2 Peter 2:3, 14–16.

---

8. Explain why pilfering or misappropriating church funds is such a powerful temptation, and a worldwide problem among churches. (For help see 1 Tim. 6:6–11; Luke 16:14.)

9. In your own words, explain what each of the following phrases mean:

a. The mystery of the faith

b. Holding to the mystery of the faith

c. With a clear conscience

> Whoever is greedy for unjust gain troubles his own household.
> (Prov. 15:27)

10. How would you briefly summarize the qualification required of a deacon in 1 Timothy 3:9?

11. A deacon's lifestyle (conduct, behavior, attitude) must match his beliefs (biblical doctrines, the gospel). There must not be a disconnect between one's conduct and beliefs. How do the following verses state this same important theme (v. 9), but use different language and imagery?

12. Also, which of the following expressions most forcefully make the point that conduct and profession must match?

  a. Ezra 7:10

  b. Matthew 23:1–3

  c. Matthew 7:21–27

  d. Luke 8:21

e. James 1:22–25; 2:26

13. Why is the qualification stated in 1 Timothy 3:9 so vital to a deacon's public reputation and work as an aide to the elders?

ADDITIONAL INFORMATION
OPTIONAL QUESTIONS AND ASSIGNMENTS

ASSIGNMENTS

Memorize 1 Timothy 3:8–9.

Protect the Church from Theft
List some practical steps you can take as a church to protect the local church and its leaders from stealing or misappropriating church money.

FUTURE ASSIGNMENT

Study Romans
Biblical deacons are required to "hold the mystery of the faith with a clear conscience" (v. 9). To be sure that you know the "mystery of the faith," I recommend that all deacons study Paul's letter to the Romans. You need to know Romans so that you are knowledgeable about the gospel message (doctrine) and living the Christian life (lifestyle).

Here is one way to master Romans: (1) Read and meditate through the letter of Romans; (2) prepare your own initial outline of the entire letter; (3) using a Study Bible or a one-volume Bible commentary, read the commentary material on Romans; (4) afterward, read a more in-depth commentary on Romans, and if need be, adjust your original outline to agree with the commentary; (5) while you are in your car (or elsewhere) listen to a Spirit-gifted Bible expositor teach through the letter of Romans. There is much free material online for listening to the Word preached by gifted expositors.

When you have completed this assignment (however long this takes) do the same thing with Paul's letter to the Ephesians.

QUESTIONS

a. Paul says in 2 Corinthians 2:11, "For we are not ignorant of [Satan's] designs." In what ways do the biblical qualifications for elders and deacons protect the local church from Satan's designs to corrupt the church morally and spiritually? Note especially 1 Timothy 3:6–7 and Ephesians 6:11–12.

b. In light of the five qualifications presented in verses 8 and 9, what kind of behaviors would a biblically qualified deacon model for the church?

c. Many churches seem either to be unaware of the biblical requirements for deacons or to be ignoring them in the selection of their deacons. What explanation can you give for this widespread problem?

The Power of the Purse

A question that often arises is, should the deacons determine the financial direction of the church's funds? I would answer, "No!" According to Titus 1:7, the overseers/elders (not the deacons or trustees) are "God's stewards" (Greek, *oikonomos*, "house manager") of God's household.

The deacons function under the pastoral oversight of the elders. The elders can call on the deacons to help administer church funds or just a portion of funds for mercy ministries. However, the final control and direction of the church's funds should be the elders' responsibility (God's stewards, Titus 1:7).

As assistants to the elders, you enter into spiritual warfare in a new, intensive way. Be aware of your adversary the devil.

Verses on the Archenemy:

"**Satan**" (Job 1:6–12; Rom. 16:20; 1 Cor. 5:5; 7:5; 2 Cor. 2:11; 11:14; 12:7; Eph. 4:27; 1 Thess. 2:18; 2 Thess. 2:9; 1 Tim. 1:20; 3:7; 5:14–15; Rev. 12:7–9); "**the god of this world**" (2 Cor. 4:4); "**Belial**" (2 Cor. 6:15); "**the prince of the power of the air**" (Eph. 2:2); "**the devil**" (John 8:44; Eph. 6:11; 1 Tim. 3:6, 7; 2 Tim. 2:26; Heb. 2:14–15; James 4:7; 1 Peter 5:8; 1 John 3:8–10; Rev. 20:10); "**the evil one**" (Eph. 6:16); "**the deceiver**" (Rev. 12:9); "**the tempter**" (Matt. 4:3; 1 Thess. 3:5); "**the adversary**" (1 Tim. 5:14; 1 Peter 5:8).

---

[1]"Double-tongued" (*dilogos*): "sincere," NIV; "not hypocritical," *Christian Standard Bible*; "insincere" (Walter Bauer, *A Greek-English Lexicon of the New Testament and Other Early Christian Literature*, 3rd ed., trans. W. F. Arndt and F. W. Gingrich, revised and edited by Frederick William Danker [Chicago: University of Chicago, 2000], 250).

Chapter 6

Examination

1 Timothy 3:10

**Before completing this lesson, read
Chapter 6 in *Paul's Vision for the Deacons*.**

And let them also be tested first; then let them serve as deacons if they prove themselves blameless. (1 Tim. 3:10)

Key Statements from Chapter 6

Without this requirement to examine whether or not a deacon candidate possesses the necessary scriptural qualities for office, the qualifications listed in verses 8–9 are just empty words on a piece of paper. (p. 106)

The Greek verb translated "tested" (*dokimazō*) means "to make a critical examination of something, to determine genuineness, put to the test, examine."[1] In ancient Greek literature, *dokimazō* was sometimes used in reference to the examination of a person's credentials for public office. (p. 107)

A proper sequence for becoming a deacon must be followed, and the examination of the candidate must come "first." If the outcome of the deacon candidate's screening is positive, "then," and only then, is the candidate eligible to serve as an assistant to the elders. (p. 108)

A deacon who is found "blameless" in this regard is worthy of respect, truthful in speech, self-controlled in the use of wine, sound in doctrine and life, and a faithful husband, good father, and competent household manager. (p. 108)

Scripture only prescribes (1) the qualifications for deacons, (2) the necessity for examination by others, and (3) the warning to avoid hasty appointments to office (1 Tim. 3:8–12; 5:22). (p. 110)

The office of deacon, like the office of elder, is a public office in the church, and the qualifications for deacons are written in Scripture for the entire church family to know and enforce. So the examination of a prospective deacon is to be a public matter, not a private decision made by a few people. (p. 112)

Whatever procedures you use to select, examine, approve, and install a prospective deacon, think them through carefully. Continue to evaluate their effectiveness and improve the process. (p. 116)

---

1. Reread the opening story of Valleyview Church. In what ways did the church and its pastor fail in appointing new deacons? List several ways in which the church failed.

2. Why must there be an examination by the church and its leaders of a deacon candidate's fitness for office? List as many reasons as you can.

3. What does the Greek word for "tested" (*dokimazō*) mean? Explain all that you now know about this key word. If you have access to Bible commentaries or dictionaries, use them to help you grasp the meaning of this word.

4. What do the sequential words "first" and "then" tell you about the process of appointing deacons to office?

Command and teach these things.

1 Timothy 4:11

Command these things as well, so that they may be without reproach.

1 Timothy 5:7

Teach and urge these things.

1 Timothy 6:2

5. What does it mean that a deacon candidate must be proven "blameless"? Is anyone blameless?

6. Who should take the lead in the process of examining and approving new deacons? How would you support your answer with Scripture?

7. What does Scripture mean when it says, "Do not be hasty in the laying on of hands, nor take part in the sins of others" (1 Tim. 5:22)? How does this principle apply to deacons? If you have access to Bible commentaries or dictionaries, use them to help you interpret verse 22.

8. Why would the elders want to involve the congregation in the examination and approval of new deacons? What Scriptures would you use to justify your answers?

9. Read Acts 6:1–7 and Acts 15:1–29. What important principles do these two passages teach you about the elder-congregation relationship and the decision-making process in the church? For help, see endnote 11 on pages 117–118 in the text.

10. Why should there be some kind of formal, public installation of a deacon before the church body?

11. What would the laying on of hands mean to the church and to the deacon if it is done at the installation of a new deacon?

12. What practical new ideas did you learn about appointing deacons from this chapter?

ADDITIONAL INFORMATION
OPTIONAL QUESTIONS AND ASSIGNMENTS

ASSIGNMENT

Memorize 1 Timothy 3:10.

Appointing Deacons

The appointment of deacons is not the same thing as the appointment of the seven almoners of Acts 6. The table-serving Seven of Acts 6 were appointed to a very specific task, supervising the church's charitable funds to widows (Acts 6:1–3). Because the table-serving Seven handled the church's charitable funds and cared for the church's widows, the apostles wanted the church to chose its own charitable officials (Acts 6:3, 5). Still the apostles did the official, public appointing of the Seven by the laying on of hands. Because of who Paul's deacons are, however, their appointment does not need to follow the same procedures as the selection and appointment of the Seven in Acts 6.

Paul's deacons are to assist the elders in whatever tasks the elders need assistance, in order to relieve the elders so that they can concentrate more fully on leading and teaching. Thus, the elders will need to take the initiative in choosing and training their assistants. But since the qualifications for deacons are listed in Scripture for all to know and enforce, the congregation will need to be involved in the examination of the deacons. Exactly how this is done is left to the discretion of the local church with its leaders.

Below is a proposed plan to consider. Adjust it as you see fit.

(1) The elders will identify their need for official assistants.

(2) The elders will identify faithful men (or an individual candidate) in the congregation who they see have the potential to be assistants.

(3) The elders can invite these potential deacons to study with them the biblical teaching of who deacons are and what they do. You can use this study guide as a tool for study or make up your own course of study.

(4) If the candidates are eager to be deacons and appear to qualify, they can be presented to the congregation for examination as to their qualifications for office. The survey at the end of this chapter can be helpful in this process.

(5) Upon examination, if the candidate is found to be qualified, the elders can state the candidates' approval and then publicly appoint him to office by the laying on of hands or any other means of pubic acknowledgment.

A Sample Deacon Evaluation Survey

[Adjust this survey to fit your church's procedures. This sample form is also available as letter-size print-out on www.deaconbook.com.]

In evaluating a deacon candidate, you are participating in one of the most important activities affecting the life and future of our church. So please carefully and prayerfully fill out this deacon qualification survey.

Please check one of the three boxes next to each qualification.

Brief Biography of the Candidate: [The evaluation form should include a brief biographical sketch, written by the candidate, that will give the evaluators information on the candidate's family, his conversion experience, date of baptism, when he joined the church, his past and current ministry involvement in the church, his personal interests, and his principal doctrinal positions and agreement with the church's distinctives. A photo of the candidate would also be helpful, particularly in larger churches.]

QUALIFICATIONS FOR: Name____	EVALUATING THE CANDIDATE'S QUALIFICATIONS		
	Qualified	Don't Know or Unable to Comment	Not Qualified
THE BIBLICAL QUALIFICATIONS			
Dignified: worthy of respect; a respectable, well-thought-of person			
Not double-tongued: integrity of speech; does not exhibit any kind of insincere or duplicitous speech			
Not addicted to much wine: above reproach in the use of alcohol; not addicted to or does not abuse alcohol			
Not greedy for dishonest gain: financial integrity; would not fleece the faithful for personal gain; does not refuse financial accountability; not dishonest with money			
Holding to the mystery of the faith with a clear conscience: adheres firmly to the Christian faith and lives consistently with the faith; lifestyle and doctrine match; not a hypocrite			
Blameless: above reproach in regard to the qualifications for the office of deacon, free from any offensive or damaging blight of character or conduct			
Husband of one wife: a faithful husband; a one-woman kind of man			
Managing his children well: a competent father, able to care for and lead his children; provides for his children financially, emotionally, and spiritually			
Managing his own household well: competent manager of his household; household is not on the verge of collapse because of mismanagement and irresponsibility			

QUALIFICATIONS FOR:

Name _____

EVALUATING THE CANDIDATE'S QUALIFICATIONS

	Qualified	Don't Know or Unable to Comment	Not Qualified
THE CANDIDATE'S WIFE (1 Tim. 3:11)			
Dignified: worthy of respect; a respectable, well-thought-of person			
Not a slanderer: not a malicious talker or gossip; does not have a reputation for freely speaking evil of others or making damaging accusations of others			
Sober-minded: possesses stable character; level-headed, balanced judgment, self-control, free from debilitating excesses			
Faithful in all things: completely trustworthy in every area of life—in her commitment to Christ and his Word, in her duty to family, in her witness to neighbors, in all relationships, and in all responsibilities to the church family.			

Any Objections: _____

_____

Special Comments: _____

_____

_____

Your Name _____

QUESTIONS

What does the laying on of hands signify in each of the following passages of Scripture? (Note carefully who does the laying on of hands and for what reason(s); often there is more than one concurrent purpose involved in the laying on of hands.)

a. Acts 6:6

b. Acts 8:14–18

c. Acts 9:10–19

d. Acts 13:1–4

e. 1 Timothy 4:14

f. 2 Timothy 1:6–7

Biblical References on Blamelessness and Holiness

It is God's will for every believer to be blameless and holy, and the church leaders are to exemplify this. See the passages below:

You therefore must be perfect, as your heavenly Father is perfect. (Matt. 5:48)

But now that you have been set free from sin and have become slaves of God, the fruit you get leads to sanctification and its end, eternal life. (Rom. 6:22)

I appeal to you therefore, brothers, by the mercies of God, to present your bodies as a living sacrifice, holy and acceptable to God, which is your spiritual worship. (Rom. 12:1)

For God's temple is holy, and you are that temple. (1 Cor. 3:17)

Since we have these promises, beloved, let us cleanse ourselves from every defilement of body and spirit, bringing holiness to completion in the fear of God. (2 Cor. 7:1)

He chose us in him before the foundation of the world, that we should be holy and blameless before him. (Eph. 1:4)

Be pure and blameless for the day of Christ. (Phil. 1:10)

That you may be blameless and innocent, children of God without blemish in the midst of a crooked and twisted generation, among whom you shine as lights in the world. (Phil. 2:15)

And you, who once were alienated and hostile in mind, doing evil deeds, he has now reconciled in his body of flesh by his death, in order to present you holy and blameless and above reproach before him. (Col. 1:22)

So that he may establish your hearts blameless in holiness before our God and Father, at the coming of our Lord Jesus with all his saints. (1 Thess. 3:13)

[He] saved us and called us to a holy calling, not because of our works but because of his own purpose and grace, which he gave us in Christ Jesus before the ages began. (2 Tim. 1:9)

But as he who called you is holy, you also be holy in all your conduct, since it is written, "You shall be holy, for I am holy." (1 Peter 1:15–16)

Other References: Eph 2:21; 5:27; Col 3:12; 1 Thess 2:10, 5:23; 2 Tim 2:21; Heb 3:1; Jude 20, 24.

---

[1]Walter Bauer, *A Greek-English Lexicon of the New Testament and Other Early Christian Literature*, 3rd ed., trans. W. F. Arndt and F. W. Gingrich, revised and edited by Frederick William Danker (Chicago: University of Chicago, 2000), 255.

Chapter 7

WIVES

1 TIMOTHY 3:11

Before completing this lesson, read
Chapter 7 in *Paul's Vision for the Deacons*.

Their wives likewise must be dignified, not slanderers, but sober-minded, faithful in all things. (1 Tim. 3:11)

Key Statements from Chapter 7

Even if 1 Timothy 3:11 addresses the deacons' wives only, women are still to be engaged in significant mercy ministries or other vibrant ministries within the church. A woman does not need to be a deacon to participate in mercy ministries or to be part of a committee organized to serve others. (p. 119)

Just as a deacon must be "dignified" (or "worthy of respect"), his wife must be "dignified." (p. 123)

A slanderer spreads lies, false rumors, malicious gossip, and innuendos, and is capable of inflicting long-term, irreparable damage on relationships and the reputations of others. (p. 125)

If the term [sober-minded] is used figuratively in verse 11 (which is here preferred), it describes a woman who is stable, self-controlled, level-headed, and free from debilitating excesses. (p. 126)

Every aspect of a deacon's wife is to be marked by faithfulness, dependability, and reliability, so that she is worthy of respect and is a blessing to the whole church. (p. 127)

If you take the women in verse 11 to be deacons, deaconesses, or women helpers, you can still apply most of the questions in this chapter to your view. The final chapter in this study guide addresses the arguments for and against the wives-of-deacons view.

1. What has been your interpretation of 1 Timothy 3:11 before you read this chapter?

2. The author lists five views of the identity of the women in 1 Timothy 3:11. In your own words, briefly list and explain these five views, demonstrating that you understand each one. Discuss each of these views with your study group.

3. Starting with the second paragraph, reread the first section of Chapter 7 (pages 119–120 in the text). The author is making a personal plea to readers who might be offended by his view that women are not deacons. What are his points in these paragraphs? Be specific.

4. Why do you think Christians should debate but not divide over the identity of the women referred to in 1 Timothy 3:11 (women, women deacons, deaconesses, helpers, wives of deacons)?

5. What does it mean that a deacon's wife is to be "dignified," or as the *New International Version* states, "worthy of respect"? If a person is deemed "worthy of respect," what does that tell you about the person?

> A good name is to be chosen rather than great riches, and favor is better than silver or gold. (Prov. 22:1)
>
> A good name is better than precious ointment. (Ecc. 1:1)

6. Part of the Old Testament holiness code for living prohibits slander and hate.

> "You shall be holy, for I the LORD your God am holy. . . . You shall not go around as a slanderer among your people and you shall not stand up against the life of your neighbor: I am the LORD. You shall not hate your brother in your heart, but you shall reason frankly with your neighbor, lest you incur sin because of him. You shall not take vengeance or bear a grudge against the sons of your own people, but you shall love your neighbor as yourself: I am the LORD." (Lev. 19:2, 16–18)

a. From the above passage, what specific behaviors does God prohibit among his people? Be sure you can explain each one of these vices to your group members.

b. From the above passage, what specific behaviors does God require of his people?

c. Why do you think these Levitical instructions are essential to the spiritual wellbeing of the local church today?

7. A deacon's wife must not have a reputation as a slanderer or a "malicious talker" (NIV). If she does have such a reputation, what problems would this cause for the church's deacons and elders? What kinds of destructive problems do slander and malicious talk create in a church?

> The words of a whisperer are like delicious morsels; they go down into the inner parts of the body. (Prov. 18:8)
>
> Whoever utters slander is a fool. (Prov. 10:18)

8. Describe a person who is "sober-minded." Why is being "sober-minded" a necessary character quality for a deacon's wife?

9. How would you describe the opposite character traits of "sober-minded"?

10. A deacon's wife is to be "faithful in all things." How would you identify a woman who is in fact "faithful in all things"? Be specific; give an example.

> A gracious woman gets honor. (Prov. 11:16)
>
> An excellent wife is the crown of her husband. (Prov. 12:4)
>
> He who finds a wife finds a good thing and obtains favor from the Lord. (Prov. 18:22)
>
> House and wealth are inherited from fathers, but a prudent wife is from the Lord. (Prov. 19:14)

11. List some practical ways in which a deacon's wife can positively influence her husband's thinking and ministry.

12. List ways in which a deacon's wife can negatively influence her husband's thinking and ministry.

13. How will you respond if your church and fellow leaders promote a view of 1 Timothy 3:11 contrary to your own?

ADDITIONAL INFORMATION
OPTIONAL QUESTIONS AND ASSIGNMENTS

ASSIGNMENT

Memorize 1 Timothy 3:11.

QUESTIONS

a. List some of the practical ways in which the virtuous wife of Proverbs 31 illustrates the biblical qualifications "dignified . . . sober-minded, faithful in all things"? Read Proverbs 31:10–31.

(i) dignified ("worthy of respect," NIV)

(ii) sober-minded

(iii) faithful in all things

b. The husband of the "excellent wife" of Proverbs 31 is respected among the elders of the city (see v. 23). What specifically does she do that enhances her husband's public reputation in the community?

Prohibitions Against Malicious Gossip, Slander, and Backbiting

There is hardly anything that hurts people more deeply than malicious gossip, false rumors, and slanderous accusations. All slanderous talk is destructive to the church family. We all need to discipline our minds to not make comments without the facts and proper witnesses. We also need to practice the principle of going directly to the source of a rumor and not just listen to others.

Tragically, many times we believe what we first hear and pass on false information to others who do the same. Mature people should know that there is another side to every story or that most rumors are only partially accurate.

A dishonest man spreads strife, and a whisperer separates close friends. (Prov. 16:28)

The words of a whisperer are like delicious morsels; they go down into the inner parts of the body. (Prov. 18:8)

The north wind brings forth rain, and a backbiting tongue, angry looks. (Prov. 25:23)

For lack of wood the fire goes out, and where there is no whisperer, quarreling ceases. . . . A lying tongue hates its victims, and a flattering mouth works ruin. (Prov. 26:20, 28)

Do not slander a servant to his master, lest he curse you, and you be held guilty. (Prov. 30:10)

But what comes out of the mouth proceeds from the heart, and this defiles a person. For out of the heart comes evil thoughts, murder, adultery, sexual immorality, theft, false witness, slander. (Matt. 15:18–19)

a. Explain Proverbs 18:17. Give one example from your own life experience of seeing the truth of Proverbs 18:17 violated.

b. Explain Proverbs 18:13. Can you give one example from your own life experience of seeing the truth of Proverbs 18:13 violated?

c. Explain Proverbs 6:19. (The full context starts in verse 16.)

d. What are the evil consequences of rumormongering or tailbearing within a church family?

Suggested Reading

Nikki Daniel, "4 Ways Elders' Wives Can Avoid Fueling Conflict" (July 17, 2017). http://www.thegospelcoalition.org/article/4-ways-elders-wives-can-avoid-fueling-conflict. Although this is written to the wives of elders, it applies also to the deacons' wives.

> For out of the abundance of the heart the mouth speaks. The good person out of his good treasure brings forth good, and the evil person out of his evil treasure brings forth evil. I tell you, on the day of judgment people will give account for every careless word they speak, for by your words you will be justified, and by your words you will be condemned. (Matt. 12:34–37)

Chapter 8

Marriage, Children, and Household

1 Timothy 3:12

Before completing this lesson, read Chapter 8 in *Paul's Vision for the Deacons*.

Let deacons each be the husband of one wife, managing their children and their own households well. (1 Tim. 3:12)

Key Statements from Chapter 8

For the first Christian churches, marital and family issues were critically important to their spiritual well-being and survival. Family issues were also essential to the believers' witness in an unfriendly society that was already suspicious of the people called "Christians." (p. 131)

"The husband of one wife" qualification is most likely a Pauline idiom emphasizing the positive virtue of fidelity in marriage. (p. 133)

A key strategy in Satan's never-ending war on God's people is the destruction of the marriages of their leaders. (p. 136)

To protect the church, God has established specific marital requirements for its elders and deacons. Therefore, the local church must insist that its leaders meet the "husband of one wife" requirement before and during their time in office. If this requirement is not enforced by the congregation and its leaders, the local church will begin a steady slide toward unbiblical marital and sexual practices. (pp. 136–137)

Even the best fathers and mothers face problems and struggles with their children. So the requirement that the deacon be a father who manages his children "well" is not a demand for perfection. Rather, it describes a father who is actively engaged in the process of wisely and properly guiding his children through life's many struggles, failures, and problems, some of which can be severe. (p. 138)

A deacon candidate needs to show good management of those who live or work under his leadership. He is to maintain harmony in the home. His household must be stable and not be on the verge of collapse because of mismanagement. (p. 141)

Just because a believing man has social status and material success does not automatically suggest that he be a candidate for the office of elder or deacon. (p. 142)

---

1. Why are marital and family issues—as defined by Scripture—so vitally important to the spiritual health of a local church? List as many reasons as you can.

2. What does the phrase "the husband of one wife" mean? What does the phrase "the husband of one wife" not mean? (At this point you may want to read a more detailed explanation of the phrase "the husband of one wife" found online at www.deaconbook.com.)

3. Why does God insist that a local church elder or deacon be "the husband of one wife"? What is so important about this qualification?

4. What will happen to a church if it does not enforce the biblical requirement that a deacon (or elder) be "the husband of one wife"?

For this is the will of God, your sanctification: that you abstain from sexual immorality; that each one of you know how to control his own body in holiness and honor, not in the passion of lust like the Gentiles who do not know God; For God has not called us for impurity, but in holiness. Therefore whoever disregards this, disregards not man but God, who gives his Holy Spirit to you.

1 Thessalonians 4:3–5, 7–8

5. What has been one of Satan's most effective strategies in destroying the Lord's work and bringing public disgrace on the local church?

6. Explain the problem addressed in Ezra 9:1–15 (see endnote 6 on pages 143–144 in the text). What essential lessons should church leaders learn from this passage?

7. List and explain three key New Testament verses that warn Christians about the dangers of sexual immorality. (For help, see endnote 7 on page 144 in the text.)

8. Why would managing or caring for one's children in a competent way be a necessary qualification for a deacon?

He who commits adultery lacks sense; he who does it destroys himself. He will get wounds and dishonor, and his disgrace will not be wiped away. (Prov. 6:32–33)

> The righteous who walks in his integrity—blessed are his children after him! (Prov. 20:7)

9. A Christian father is not to provoke his children to anger (Eph. 6:4; Col. 3:21). In what specific ways can a father unnecessarily "provoke" his children to anger? Why does it matter if a father provokes his children to anger?

> Discipline your son, for there is hope. (Prov. 19:18)

10. Specifically, what does it mean to be a "teaching father"? Can you give an example from your own life?

11. Why is it important for a Christian father to be a teaching father?

12. If you had to judge whether or not a deacon candidate manages his household well, what specifically would you look for?

Additional Information
Optional Questions and Assignments

Assignments

Memorize 1 Timothy 3:12.

Suggested Reading

Andreas J. Köstenberger, *God, Marriage, and Family: Rebuilding the Biblical Foundation*, 2nd ed. (Wheaton, IL: Crossway, 2010). This is a great reference book needed by all elders and deacons.

Questions

God's Design for Marriage

Marriage as God intended is breathtakingly beautiful in its design. From the first three chapters of Genesis, and from our Lord's own teaching, we know that marriage was divinely instituted by a good God for the blessing and pleasure of humanity. God created the human race male and female and designed marriage to be a unique, one-flesh relationship of the two. (*Paul's Vision for the Deacons*, pages 134–135)

a. After reading pages 134–135 in the text, and especially Andreas J. Köstenberger's definition of marriage, what are some of the unique teachings of the Bible on marriage and the family that every elder and deacon need to know well? Give Scripture references.

b. What kinds of practical things do you think a busy deacon can do to protect his marriage and family from Satan's attacks to destroy marriage and family by over-business and over-work?

Know the "Sayings of the Wise" (Prov. 24:23)

As a husband and father, it is important that you know the book of Proverbs. It is full of divine wisdom for husbands and fathers.

When you have time, read through the book of Proverbs and list all the verses that speak of husband-wife relationships and father-child relationships. Also list any verses that you think will help you be a better deacon, a better assistant to the elders. Make it your goal to be a wise person.

Barbara Decker's book *Proverbs for Parenting: A Topical Guide for Child Raising from the Book of Proverbs* (Lynn's Bookshelf, 1991) is a good book for parents. The book puts the proverbs into topical categories for easy subject reference. The book is available using the *New International Version* and the *King James Version*.

Blessed is the one who finds wisdom, and the one who gets understanding, for the gain from her is better than gain from silver and her profit better than gold. She is more precious than jewels, and nothing you desire can compare with her. Long life is in her right hand; in her left hand are riches and honor. Her ways are ways of pleasantness, and all her paths are peace. She is a tree of life to those who lay hold of her; those who hold her fast are called blessed. (Prov. 3:13–18)

Get wisdom; get insight; do not forget, and do not turn away from the words of my mouth. Do not forsake her, and she will keep you; love her, and she will guard you. The beginning of wisdom is this: Get wisdom, and whatever you get, get insight. Prize her highly, and she will exalt you; she will honor you if you embrace her. She will place on your head a graceful garland; she will bestow on you a beautiful crown. (Prov. 4:5–9)

"Hear instruction and be wise, and do not neglect it. Blessed is the one who listens to me, watching daily at my gates, waiting beside my doors. For whoever finds me finds life and obtains favor from the Lord, but he who fails to find me injures himself; all who hate me love death." (Prov. 8:33–36)

How much better to get wisdom than gold! To get understanding is to be chosen rather than silver. (Prov. 16:16)

The teaching of the wise is a fountain of life, that one may turn away from the snares of death. (Prov. 13:14)

Buy truth, and do not sell it; buy wisdom, instruction, and understanding. (Prov. 23:23)

Whoever walks with the wise becomes wise. (Prov. 13:20)

The fear of the Lord is instruction in wisdom, and humility comes before honor. (Prov. 15:33)

Chapter 9

REWARDS

1 TIMOTHY 3:13

**Before completing this lesson, read
Chapter 9 in *Paul's Vision for the Deacons*.**

For those who serve well as deacons gain a good standing for themselves and also great confidence in the faith that is in Christ Jesus. (1 Tim. 3:13)

Key Statement from Chapter 9

Any idea that deacons are insignificant, or that their qualifications are not as necessary as those required of the elders, is hereby dispelled. Positive rewards await the deacons who perform their duties well. All deacons need to know these God-given, encouraging promises of rewards. (pp. 145–146)

The adverb "well," which modifies "serve," indicates commendable performance in serving as an assistant. It is not "perfunctory office bearing"[1] that is commendable, but diligent service that is rewarded. (p. 146)

To gain "a good standing" is to be held in high regard by the believing community and to be recognized and appreciated by the church family. (p. 147)

The first reward was people-focused—a good standing in the eyes of the congregation. The second reward is Christ-focused—a deeper personal faith in Christ and a closer relationship with Christ Jesus. (p. 148)

Could deacons gain anything better than great confidence in their personal faith relationship with Christ, growing deeper and closer to their Savior and Lord? (p. 151)

1. What is the connection in purpose between 1 Timothy 3:1 and 1 Timothy 3:13?

2. What do these verses (vv. 1, 13) say to those who think the deacons are an insignificant body of church officials?

3. What does serving "well" as a deacon look like?

4. What does Paul mean by "gain[ing] a good standing for themselves"? Be specific.

5. How is Paul using the prepositional phrase "in faith" in verse 13? (In Greek, the phrase literally reads, *en pistei*, "in faith.")

6. How is Paul using the prepositional phrase "in Christ Jesus" in verse 13? (In Greek, the phrase literally reads, *tē en Christō Iēsou*, "the one in Christ Jesus.")

7. Now that you have answered the two previous questions, what does Paul mean by the promise of gaining "great confidence in the faith that is in Christ Jesus"? It is important that you clearly understand this reward for good service.

8. Why is "faith" essential to a believer's relationship with Christ? Can you list any verses that support your answer?

9. What difference will it make to a deacon and his work if he significantly increases his confidence in his faith in Christ?

10. As a deacon, how does Paul's powerful conclusion in verse 13 encourage you to serve more diligently as a deacon?

11. Explain the following quotation by William Mounce and how it applies to you:

> It is not so much that by being a good deacon a person will receive rewards; it is in the actual doing of the service that one daily acquires a better standing before the people and more confidence in one's personal faith. These rewards are not given to a believer at a certain time but rather are achieved during the process of service.[2]

12. The Bible says: "Do not be slothful in zeal, be fervent in spirit, serve the Lord" (Rom. 12:11). Leon Morris elaborates on this text in the following way:

Do not be slothful in zeal: "Paul is telling the Romans that where zeal is needed they must not be lazy people."[3]

Be fervent in spirit: "It is important that the human spirit be on fire, but Paul is not referring to something that occurs by some natural process but as a result of the indwelling Spirit of God."[4]

Serve the Lord: "The verb points to thoroughgoing devotion, service like that of a slave. There is nothing half-hearted about it."[5]

Explain how each of the verses below challenges a deacon to be diligent in his work of assisting the elders with the care of God's church.

a. Ecclesiastes 9:10

b. Proverbs 18:9 and 10:26

c. Romans 12:15–16

d. 1 Corinthians 15:58

e. Colossians 3:23–24

f. Colossians 4:17

g. Hebrews 6:10–11

ADDITIONAL INFORMATION
OPTIONAL QUESTIONS AND ASSIGNMENTS

ASSIGNMENT

Memorize 1 Timothy 3:13.

QUESTIONS

Spiritual Laziness Versus Spiritual Diligence

Christians are not to be spiritually lazy or barren fruit trees. They are to "bear much fruit" for their heavenly Father (Matt. 13:23; John 15:1–8; Rom. 6:22). Yet, spiritual laziness characterizes many Christians. They do not read or study the Scriptures; they neglect to pray and have little interest in serving others; they are careless and thoughtless about their Christian responsibilities. Explain how each of the verses below warns a deacon to be aware of the sinful and destructive nature of laziness, especially spiritual laziness.

a. Proverbs 18:9

b. Proverbs 10:26

c. Proverbs 12:24

d. Proverbs 24:30–34

e. Proverbs 26:13–14

> Do not be a time waster! Pray this prayer regularly:
> "Teach us to number our days that we may get a heart of wisdom." (Ps. 90:12)

People Business

I want to end this chapter on an extremely important note. Elders and deacons are in the people business. They care for God's people. So it is vital to their work that they love the people, know the people, are friendly, approachable, out-reaching, involved, compassionate and never stand-offish, unfriendly, uninvolved, or indifferent to people.

a. Elders or deacons cannot do their work without Spirit-imparted, Christlike love. D. L. Moody, the famous 19th century evangelist said, "There is no use trying to do church work without love. A doctor, a lawyer, may do good work without love, but God's work cannot be done without love."[6] What specifically does 1 Corinthians 12:31–13:7 teach you about your ministry as an assistant to the elders and your tasks within the congregation?

b. Do not be an invisible deacon. What can you do practically to improve your presence and influence within the congregation? To understand the importance of your presence among the people, see my message on the presence of the shepherd among the sheep: http://biblicaleldership.com/effective-shepherding-172/leading-gods-flock-0/urgent-call-shepherd/elders-presence/.

Do not be *an invisible deacon.*

---

c. I have met elders and deacons who are simply not friendly or outwardly interested in people. How can you practically display a friendly and concerned attitude toward the people in your church?

d. How does the parable of the sheep and goats (Matt. 25:31–46) motivate and encourage you in your work of helping God's people.

A Deacon Bibliography

For a full bibliography of deacon books, visit www.deaconbook. com.

---

[1]George W. Knight III, *The Pastoral Epistles: A Commentary on the Greek Text*, New International Greek Testament Commentary (Grand Rapids: Eerdmans, 1992), 173.
[2]William D. Mounce, *Pastoral Epistles*, Word Biblical Commentary (Nashville, TN: Thomas Nelson, 2000), 205.
[3]Leon Morris, *The Epistle to the Romans*, Pillar New Testament Commentary (Grand Rapids: Eerdmans, 1988), 446.
[4]Morris, *Romans*, 446.
[5]Morris, *Romans*, 447.
[6]Richard Ellsworth Day, *Bush Aglow: The Life Story of Dwight Lyman Moody, Commoner of Northfield* (Philadelphia: Judson Press, 1936), 146.

Appendix

THE DEACONS' WIVES

> **Before completing this lesson, read
> the Appendix in *Paul's Vision for the Deacons*.**

Their wives likewise must be dignified, not slanderers, but sober-
minded, faithful in all things. (1 Tim. 3:11)

Gynē/Gynaikes

Gynē = woman/wife (pronounced goo-NAY)

Gynaikes = women/wives (the nominative plural of *gynē*, pronounced goo-NAI-kes)

Gynaikas = women/wives (the accusatie plural of *gynē*, prounounced goo-NAI-kas)

In Chapter 7, we listed five major views of the women (*gynaikas*) in verse 11:

(1) All Christian women in general
(2) Women deacons (coequals with male deacons)
(3) Deaconesses (a third, separate office, not coequals with male deacons)
(4) Women helpers, or assistants to the deacons
(5) Wives of the deacons

To help bring clarity and consistency to this subject, the term *woman deacon* is used to describe the second view above, and the term *deaconess* to describe the third view. Be aware that some commentators use *deaconess* to mean *woman deacon*. There is considerable inconsistency and confusion in how the different commentators use these terms.

The questions in this chapter are of a technical nature and may be difficult. You may find it more profitable to study this chapter, preparing your answers, with the help of someone else. If you would like to study this issue more in depth, or would like to help your group consider more in-depth arguments, go online to www. deaconbook.com.

1. The author states that, "How people view the office of deacon will be a significant factor in interpreting who the *gynaikes* of verse 11 are." Explain how the author's view of the identity and role of the deacon affects his interpretation of the women of verse 11.

2. Explain the problem that the Greek word *gynaikas* in 1 Timothy 3:11 creates for the Bible translator or commentator. How does your Bible handle the translation of this term? Do you agree or disagree with your Bible translation?

3. In verse 11, Paul uses the Greek word *gynaikas* (women/wives) rather than a more specific title, e.g., *tas diakonous* or *gynaikas diakonous* (women deacons). As best as you can, explain why the author sees this as a problem.

4. All the arguments the author uses can be answered by counter-arguments. How would you refute the author's interpretation of verse 11? (For help go to www.deaconbook.com or a Bible commentary.)

5. Explain the point of the argument of the placement of *gynaikas* (v. 11) in the midst of male deacons. How would you refute the author's point? (For help go to www.deaconbook.com or a Bible commentary.)

6. Read again the section, "The Omission of Any Marital or Family Requirements" (see pages 161–162 in the text). What is the point of the writer's argument and why does he make a big point of this argument? How would you refute this argument?

7. In what ways are the five qualifications for the male deacons (vv. 8–9) and the four qualifications for the women (v. 11) similar and dissimilar? List them below.

8. How would you refute those who argue that the similar (or same) qualifications of the women in verse 11 with the male deacons in verses 8–10 demonstrate that they are women deacons?

<u>Similar</u>   <u>Dissimilar</u>

9. Another point of contention is the interpretation of Romans 16:1. Phoebe is called a *diakonos*.

a. What problems do all interpreters face when trying to interpret the term *diakonos* in Romans 16:1?

b. What is your suggestion for solving this interpretive problem? (For help go to www.deaconbook.com or a Bible commentary.)

10. One key criticism of the wives-of-the-deacons view is the omission of the pronoun (their) or the article (the) with *gynaikas.* This is a legitimate criticism.

  a. How does the author answer this objection?

  b. Do you think the author has adequately answered this criticism? Explain.

11. Another objection to the wives-of-the-deacons view claims that the content and particularly the grammatical structure of the passage requires that the women of verse 11 to be equally officeholders with the male deacons.

  Verse 2: Therefore an overseer must be (*dei* . . . *einai*) above reproach.
  Verse 8: Deacons likewise [must be] dignified; ("must be" is supplied from verse 2).
  Verse 11: Women likewise [must be] dignified; ("must be" is supplied from verse 2).

  a. How does the author answer the above objection?

  b. Do you think the author has adequately answered this objection? Explain.

12. A final objection asks, if the deacons' wives must be of a certain godly character, should not such requirements be even more necessary for the elders' wives? Some argue that the absence of a list of specific qualifications for the elders' wives in verses 2–7 is another key indicator that verse 11 refers to women deacons, deaconesses, or helpers.

    a. How does the author answer this objection?

    b. Do you think the author has adequately answered this objection? Explain.

13. What do you think are the two strongest arguments the author presents in the Appendix in favor of the wives-of-the-deacons view? Explain your answer.

14. What do you think is the strongest objection to the wives-of-the-deacons view?

FINAL RECOMMENDATIONS, QUESTIONS, AND DISCUSSIONS

Before trying to change the structure of your church's deacons (or anything else for that matter), first work diligently at teaching the congregation the "more excellent way" of behaving, the way of Christlike love (1 Cor. 12:31). In other words, labor at setting the right Christian tone for your church. "Let all that you do be done in love" (1 Cor. 16:14). If you, as leaders, set the right attitudes for the church, the Christlike attitudes (Phil. 2:2–8), your church will be able to make changes in a more constructive way. If your church is characterized by prideful, fleshly attitudes, any changes you try to make will result in conflict and division (1 Cor. 3:1–4; 2 Cor. 12:20; Gal. 5:20, 26; James 3:14–16). So before changing the structure of your deacons (or elders), have the church read and study the following books. Or, you can use these books and teach what is in them to the congregation.

Agape Leadership: Lessons in Spiritual Leadership from the Life of R. C. Chapman (an easy 80 pages of reading)

Love or Die: Christ's Wake-up Call to the Church (70 pages)

If You Bite and Devour One Another: Biblical Principles for Handling Conflict (162 pages of reading)

I have written the above books with the purpose of setting right Christian attitudes and behaviors in the church, the Christlike attitudes (Phil. 2:2–8). Paul did the same for the troubled churches he wrote to (Rom. 12:9–21; 13:8–10; 1 Cor. 12:31–14:1; 16:14; 2 Cor. 2:4; Gal. 5:22; 6:2; Eph. 4:2, 16; Phil. 2:2–8; Col. 3:12–14; 1 Thess. 4:9–10; 5:13; 1 Tim. 1:5).

QUESTIONS

a. As church leaders and teachers, what can you do to make sure that your congregation knows well the Christlike attitudes and behaviors that should characterize all that they do and say?

b. What parts of this book did you agree with? What parts did you disagree with?

c. How much agreement is there among your elders or deacons regarding the arguments of this book? To what degree are you divided over the issues of this book?

d. If you, as elders or deacons, agree with the conclusion of this book, or partially agree, who will take the lead in implementing the principles of this book? What would need to change in your church in order to better align with the conclusions of this book?

e. Are there any current deacons who are not biblically qualified that need to be removed from office? How would you remove them from office without disapproving of them as Christian servants?

---

[1]Another book aimed at leaders is *A Christian Leader's Guide to Leading with Love* (Littleton, CO: Lewis and Roth, 2006).